Learn Italian For Beginners

The Ultimate Italian Language Learning Guide For Beginners. Learn Beginner Italian Step by Step With Fast Track Tips That Will Help You Speak Italian With Confidence.

Laura Mancini

Table of Contents

1. Introduction 1
2. General terms 4
   2.1 Essentials and conversation 4
   2.2 Pronouns and referring to people 16
   2.3 Days of the week and time expressions 22
   2.4 Months and seasons 30
3. Health 35
   3.1 Emergencies 35
4. Going places 39
5. Accomodation 48
   5.1 Looking for accommodation 48
6. Eating out 50
   6.1 Ordering food 50
   6.2 Ordering drinks 56

Conclusions 60

1. Introduction

Traveling doesn't just mean visiting monuments, spending hours in museums or going to restaurants to taste local food. People are the most important factor in a nation and traveling without interacting or trying to speak directly with locals will make your experience somewhat incomplete.

Before leaving, you can commit yourself to learning some useful words and phrases in Italian so that you can get to know the Italian population, make small conversations or simply surprise and delight the locals with your knowledge of the most famous national pride: their language

There is nothing you can do that will increase the pleasure of traveling more than learning the essential phrases in all the countries you travel to.

Locals around the world are in most cases friendly and, without a doubt, knowing the key phrases in a foreign language will allow you to make friends without too many efforts.

Tips and tricks on how to make sure you are understood:

1. Don't be afraid to mispronounce words.

2. Don't be afraid to try, or ask a local person to give you advices on the pronunciation of certain words.

3. Knowing key phrases in a foreign language will help you meet people.

4. Saying verbs improperly is fine.

5. While traveling, try learning three new words a day. Write them to memorize them perfectly. By the end of your trip, you will manage to learn many new words.

6. If a language uses a different alphabet, write the words phonetically (the way you'd listen to them).

7. While traveling, don't expect everyone to know English.

8. Learning a new alphabet is not that difficult. The Cyrillic alphabet, the Persian alphabet or the Arabic alphabet can be learned in one full day of heavy learning.

9. Learn the numbers

10. To memorize a word, repeat mentally 30 times and orally 30 times. This will probably be enough for a word to stick to your consciousness. Otherwise, do it again.

11. Learn how to greet people.

12. It is always good to mix words and hand gestures to make other people understand you.

13. People are often a mirror of yourself. Your friendliness in most cases reflects in them (even if they have had a bad day).

14. Never make fun of someone who speaks a bad English. It means that they know another language or probably more than one.

15. Learn to say yes, no, and maybe.

16. Always smile and be genuinely happy to meet people.

17. Accept an invitation to do something with someone who does not speak English, and even if you know only a few necessary words in the language.

18. A lunch at someone's home to meet the family and have a local meal will be the best way to learn a few more words.

Good reasons to learn Italian

Knowing Italian will make your trip in Italy completely different. It will become possible for you to travel outside the traditional tourist circuits and to mix with the locals, avoiding the usual hotels and tourist villages. Of course, this can be a source of anxiety and fear, but don't worry because as soon as you get close and try to communicate with the locals, you will immediately realize how open and friendly they are, and you will immediately calm down. In this way, you will experience much more interesting and exciting travel adventures.

By learning the main words and sentences of the Italian language, you will have the opportunity to meet new people from all over the world and often to establish friendships that will last even after returning home, thanks to social media and the chance of visiting each other's countries of origin.

It can be the first step into living, working and studying abroad. For example, have you ever dreamed of living on a beautiful Italian island? Would you like to go to study in a big city such as Milan or Palermo? Well, learning Italian can open the door to these possibilities. And along the way you may even come across the partner or job of your dreams!

Nowadays, if you want to find a great job or are planning to pursue an important career, you need to speak at least two languages. In a globalized world, most companies operate more and more internationally and in fact require that their employees have extensive language skills in order to be able to communicate with people all over the world. In addition, a survey showed that employees with excellent language skills often have a higher salary than others. So, speaking a foreign language is the way to success in work, love and life. What more could you ask for?

2. General terms

Even if you are not interested in becoming the latest Italian language expert, a few general terms will help you get around much quicker and experience your adventure in a much more profound way. Do not forget, furthermore, that not everyone in Italy speaks fluent English, so if you should need help with something, knowing a couple of words will be very helpful.

2.1 Essentials and conversation

English: Hi!

Italian: *Salve!*

Repeat: *Salve!*

Spell: *S-a-l-v-e!*

Use it in a phrase: Salve, posso entrare? *Hi, can I come in?*
Repeat: Salve, posso entrare? *Hi, can I come in?*

English: Hi!

Italian: *Ciao!*

Repeat: *Ciao!*

Spell: *C-i-a-o!*

Use it in a phrase: Ciao, come stai? *Hi, how are you?*
Repeat: Ciao, come stai? *Hi, how are you?*

English: Good morning!

Italian: *Buongiorno!*

Repeat: *Buongiorno!*

Spell: *B-u-o-n-g-i-o-r-n-o!*

Use it in a phrase: Buongiorno, entra pure! *Hi, come on in!*

Repeat: Buongiorno, entra pure! *Hi, come on in!*

English: Good evening!

Italian: *Buona sera!*

Repeat: *Buona sera!*

Spell: *B-u-o-n-a-s-e-r-a!*

Use it in a phrase: Buonasera e benvenuto! *Good evening and welcome!*
Repeat: Buonasera e benvenuto! *Good evening and welcome!*

English: Goodnight!

Italian: *Buona notte!*

Repeat: *Buona notte!*

Spell: *B-u-o-n-a-n-o-t-t-e*

Use it in a phrase: Buonanotte, a domani! *Good night, see you tomorrow!*
Repeat: Buonanotte, a domani! *Good night, see you tomorrow!*

English: How are you?

Italian: Come va?

Repeat: *Come va?*

Spell: *C-o-m-e v-a?*

Use it in a phrase: Ciao, come va? *Hi, how are you?*
Repeat: Ciao, come va? *Hi, how are you?*

English: Good, thanks.

Italian: Bene, grazie.

Repeat: Bene, grazie.

Spell: *B-e-n-e, g-r-a-z-i-e!*

Use it in a phrase: Bene, grazie! E tu? *Good, thanks! And you?*
Repeat: Bene, grazie! E tu? *Good, thanks! And you?*

English: What's your name?

Italian: Come ti chiami?

Repeat: Come ti chiami?

Spell: *C-o-m-e t-i c-h-i-a-m-i?*

Use it in a phrase: Io sono Luca, come ti chiami? *I am Luca, what's your name?*
Repeat: Io sono Luca, come ti chiami? *I am Luca, what's your name?*

English: My name is ____

Italian: *Mi chiamo* ____

Repeat: *Mi chiamo* ____

Spell: *M-i c-h-i-a-m-o* ____

Use it in a phrase: Mi chiamo Maria, piacere! *My name is Maria, nice to meet you!*
Repeat: Mi chiamo Maria, piacere! *My name is Maria, nice to meet you!*

English: Where do you come from?

Italian: *Da dove vieni?*

Repeat: *Da dove vieni?*

Spell: *D-a d-o-v-e v-i-e-n-i?*

Use it in a phrase: Ciao Marco, da dove vieni? *Hi Marco, where do you come from?*
Repeat: Ciao Marco, da dove vieni? *Hi Marco, where do you come from?*

English: I come from ____

Italian: *Vengo da* ____

Repeat: *Vengo da* ____

Spell: *V-e-n-g-o d-a* ____

Use it in a phrase: *Vengo da Napoli.* *I come from Naples.*
Repeat: *Vengo da Napoli.* *I come from Naples.*

English: How old are you?

Italian: *Quanti anni hai?*

Repeat: *Quanti anni hai?*

Spell: *Q-u-a-n-t-i a-n-n-i h-a-i?*

Use it in a phrase: *Sei giovane, quanti anni hai?* *You are young, how old are you?*
Repeat: *Sei giovane, quanti anni hai?* *You are young, how old are you?*

English: I am ____ old.

Italian: *Ho ___ anni.*

Repeat: *Ho ___ anni.*

Spell: *H-o ___ a-n-n-i.*

Use it in a phrase: *Non sono giovane, ho 45 anni.* *I am not young, I am 45 years old.*
Repeat: *Non sono giovane, ho 45 anni.* *I am not young, I am 45 years old.*

English: Yes.

Italian: *Si.*

Repeat: *Si.*

Spell: *S-i.*

Use it in a phrase: Non credi? Si. *Don't you think? Yes.*
Repeat: Non credi? Si. *Don't you think? Yes.*

English: No.

Italian: *No.*

Repeat: *No.*

Spell: *N-o.*

Use it in a phrase: Vieni anche tu? No. *Are you coming too? No.*
Repeat: Vieni anche tu? No. *Are you coming too? No.*

English: Please

Italian: *Per favore*

Repeat: *Per favore*

Spell: *P-e-r f-a-v-o-r-e*

Use it in a phrase: Mi passi il pane, per favore? *Can I have the bread, please?*
Repeat: Mi passi il pane, per favore? *Can I have the bread, please?*

English: Here it is!

Italian: *Ecco qui!*

Repeat: *Ecco qui!*

Spell: *E-c-c-o q-u-i!*

Use it in a phrase: Ecco qui il pane! *Here is the bread!*
Repeat: Ecco qui il pane! *Here is the bread!*

English: Thank you

Italian: *Grazie*

Repeat: *Grazie*

Spell: *G-r-a-z-i-e*

Use it in a phrase: Grazie, non dovevi! *Thank you, you shouldn't have!*
Repeat: Grazie, non dovevi! *Thank you, you shouldn't have!*

English: *Thank you very much*

Italian: *Grazie mille*

Repeat: *Grazie mille*

Spell: *G-r-a-z-i-e m-i-l-l-e*

Use it in a phrase: Grazie mille per l'informazione! *Thank you very much for the information!*
Repeat: Grazie mille per l'informazione! *Thank you very much for the information!*

English: You are welcome

Italian: *Prego*

Repeat: *Prego*

Spell: *P-r-e-g-o*

Use it in a phrase: Prego, quando vuoi! *You are welcome, whenever!*
Repeat: Prego, quando vuoi! *You are welcome, whenever!*

English: No problem

Italian: *Non c'è di che*

Repeat: *Non c'è di che*

Spell: N-o-n c'-è d-i c-h-e

Use it in a phrase: Non c'è di che, spero ti piaccia! *No problem, I hope you like it!*

Repeat: Non c'è di che, spero ti piaccia! *No problem, I hope you like it!*

English: I am sorry

Italian: *Mi dispiace*

Repeat: *Mi dispiace*

Spell: M-i d-i-s-p-i-a-c-e

Use it in a phrase: Mi dispiace, colpa mia! *I am sorry, my bad!*
Repeat: Mi dispiace, colpa mia! *I am sorry, my bad!*

English: Excuse me

Italian: *Mi scusi*

Repeat: *Mi scusi*

Spell: M-i s-c-u-s-i

Use it in a phrase: Mi scusi, non l'avevo vista! *I am sorry, I didn't see you there!*
Repeat: Mi scusi, non l'avevo vista! *I am sorry, I didn't see you there!*

English: No problem

Italian: *Niente*

Repeat: *Niente*

Spell: N-i-e-n-t-e

Use it in a phrase: Niente, non ti preoccupare! *No problem, don't worry!*
Repeat: Niente, non ti preoccupare! *No problem, don't worry!*

English: Warning!

Italian: *Attenzione!*

Repeat: *Attenzione!*

Spell: A-t-t-e-n-z-i-o-n-e!

Use it in a phrase: Attenzione allo scalino! *Careful to the step!*
Repeat: Attenzione allo scalino! *Careful to the step!*

English: I'm hungry

Italian: *Ho fame*

Repeat: *Ho fame*

Spell: H-o f-a-m-e

Use it in a phrase: Ho fame, pranziamo? *I am hungry, let's have lunch?*
Repeat: Ho fame, pranziamo? *I am hungry, let's have lunch?*

English: I am thirsty

Italian: *Ho sete*

Repeat: *Ho sete*

Spell: H-o s-e-t-e

Use it in a phrase: Ho sete, hai dell'acqua? *I am thirsty, do you have any water?*
Repeat: Ho sete, hai dell'acqua? *I am thirsty, do you have any water?*

English: I am tired

Italian: *Sono stanco*

Repeat: *Sono stanco*

Spell: S-o-n-o s-t-a-n-c-o

Use it in a phrase: Sono stanco, vado a dormire! *I am tired, I am going to sleep*
Repeat: Sono stanco, vado a dormire! *I am tired, I am going to sleep*

English: I am not feeling good

Italian: *Mi sento poco bene*

Repeat: *Mi sento poco bene*

Spell: M-i s-e-n-t-o p-o-c-o b-e-n-e

Use it in a phrase: Mi sento poco bene, chiama il dottore! *I am not feeling good, call the doctor!*
Repeat: Mi sento poco bene, chiama il dottore! *I am not feeling good, call the doctor!*

English: I don't know

Italian: *Non lo so*

Repeat: *Non lo so*

Spell: N-o-n l-o s-o

Use it in a phrase: Non lo so, non sono Italiana! *I don't know, I am not Italian*
Repeat: Non lo so, non sono Italiana! *I don't know, I am not Italian*

English: It was nice meeting you

Italian: *è stato un piacere conoscerti*

Repeat: *è stato un piacere conoscerti*

Spell: è s-t-a-t-o u-n p-i-a-c-e-r-e c-o-n-o-s-c-e-r-t-i

Use it in a phrase: è stato un piacere conoscerti, alla prossima! *It was nice meeting you, see you next time*
Repeat: è stato un piacere conoscerti, alla prossima! *It was nice meeting you, see you next time*

English: Goodbye

Italian: *Arrivederci*

Repeat: Arrivederci

Spell: A-r-r-i-v-e-d-e-r-c-i

Use it in a phrase: Vado a casa, arrivederci! *I am going home, goodbye!*
Repeat: Vado a casa, arrivederci! *I am going home, goodbye!*

English: I am American/ Canadian/ British

Italian: *Sono Americano/ Canadese/ Inglese*

Repeat: *Sono Americano/ Canadese/ Inglese*

Spell: S-o-n-o A-m-e-r-i-c-a-n-o/ C-a-n-a-d-e-s-e/ I-n-g-l-e-s-e

Use it in a phrase: Non sono Italiano, sono Americano/ Canadese/ Inglese! *I am not Italian, I am American/ Canadian/ British*
Repeat: Non sono Italiano, sono Americano/ Canadese/ Inglese! *I am not Italian, I am American/ Canadian/ British*

English: Nice to meet you

Italian: *Piacere*

Repeat: *Piacere*

Spell: P-i-a-c-e-r-e

Use it in a phrase: Piacere, mi chiamo Laura *Nice to meet you, my name is Laura*
Repeat: Piacere, mi chiamo Laura *Nice to meet you, my name is Laura*

English: I am sorry, I don't understand

Italian: *Mi scusi, non capisco*

Repeat: *Mi scusi, non capisco*

Spell: M-i s-c-u-s-i, n-o-n c-a-p-i-s-c-o

Use it in a phrase: Mi scusi, non capisco l'Italiano. *I am sorry, I don't understand Italian*
Repeat: Mi scusi, non capisco l'Italiano. *I am sorry, I don't understand Italian*

English: I don't speak Italian

Italian: *Non parlo Italiano*

Repeat: *Non parlo Italiano*

Spell: N-o-n p-a-r-l-o I-t-a-l-i-a-n-o

Use it in a phrase: Non parlo Italiano, parlo Inglese. *I don't speak Italian, I speak English.*
Repeat: Non parlo Italiano, parlo Inglese. *I don't speak Italian, I speak English.*

English: Can you repeat, please?

Italian: *Puoi ripetere, per favore?*

Repeat: *Puoi ripetere, per favore?*

Spell: P-u-o-i r-i-p-e-t-e-r-e p-e-r f-a-v-o-r-e?

Use it in a phrase: Non ho capito, puoi ripetere per favore? *I didn't understand, can you repeat please?*
Repeat: Non ho capito, puoi ripetere per favore? *I didn't understand, can you repeat please?*

English: What does it mean?

Italian: Cosa vuol dire?

Repeat: Cosa vuol dire?

Spell: C-o-s-a v-u-o-l d-i-r-e?

Use it in a phrase: Cosa vuol dire questa parola? *What does this word mean?*
Repeat: Cosa vuol dire questa parola? *What does this word mean?*

English: Do you speak English?

Italian: *Parla Inglese?*

Repeat: *Parla Inglese?*

Spell: P-a-r-l-a I-n-g-l-e-s-e?

Use it in a phrase: Non parlo Italiano, parla inglese? *I don't speak Italian, do you speak English?*
Repeat: Non parlo Italiano, parla inglese? *I don't speak Italian, do you speak English?*

English: It doesn't matter

Italian: *Non importa*

Repeat: *Non importa*

Spell: N-o-n i-m-p-o-r-t-a

Use it in a phrase: Non importa, per me va bene. *It doesn't matter, to me it's fine.*
Repeat: Non importa, per me va bene. *It doesn't matter, to me it's fine.*

English: May I come in?

Italian: *Permesso?*

Repeat: *Permesso?*

Spell: P-e-r-m-e-s-s-o?

Use it in a phrase: Permesso, posso entrare? *May I come in?*
Repeat: Permesso, posso entrare? *May I come in?*

2.2 Pronouns and referring to people

The one major difference between English and Italian pronouns is that in Italy, the pronoun corresponding to *she (lei)* is also used as *you*, in a formal context. It could be used to refer to someone older than you, a teacher or a professional, or simply someone you don't know and whom you wish to be respectful.

An interesting fact to know about this is that in archaic Italian, and sometimes today in the deep south of Italy, the word for *you – plural- (voi)* is used to pay absolute respect to someone. It is even more formal than the aforementioned *lei*.

English: I

Italian: *Io*

Repeat: *Io*

Spell: I-o

Use it in a phrase: Io sono Tedesco. *I am German*
Repeat: Io sono Tedesco. *I am German*

English: You

Italian: *Tu*

Repeat: *Tu*

Spell: T-u

Use it in a phrase: Tu sei fidanzato? *Do you have a girlfriend?*
Repeat: Tu sei fidanzato? *Do you have a girlfriend?*

English: You

Italian: *Lei*

Repeat: *Lei*

Spell: L-e-i

Use it in a phrase: Lei è un dottore? *Are you a doctor?*

Repeat: Lei è un dottore? *Are you a doctor?*

English: He

Italian: *Lui*

Repeat: *Lui*

Spell: L-u-i

Use it in a phrase: Lui è tuo fratello? *Is he your brother?*
Repeat: Lui è tuo fratello? *Is he your brother?*

English: She

Italian: *Lei*

Repeat: *Lei*

Spell: L-e-i

Use it in a phrase: Lei è la sua migliore amica *She is her bestfriend*
Repeat: Lei è la sua migliore amica *She is her bestfriend*

English: We

Italian: *Noi*

Repeat: *Noi*

Spell: N-o-i

Use it in a phrase: Noi siamo i suoi genitori *We are her parents*
Repeat: Noi siamo i suoi genitori *We are her parents*

English: You (plural)

Italian: *Voi*

Repeat: *Voi*

Spell: V-o-i

Use it in a phrase: Voi siete sposati? *Are you married?*

Repeat: Voi siete sposati? *Are you married?*

English: They
Italian: *Loro*

Repeat: *Loro*

Spell: L-o-r-o

Use it in a phrase: Loro se ne vanno ora *They are leaving now.*
Repeat: Loro se ne vanno ora *They are leaving now.*

English: Person
Italian: *Persona*

Repeat: *Persona*

Spell: P-e-r-s-o-n-a

Use it in a phrase: è una bella persona *She is a beautiful person*
Repeat: è una bella persona *She is a beautiful person*

English: Man
Italian: *Uomo*

Repeat: *Uomo*

Spell: U-o-m-o

Use it in a phrase: è un uomo molto alto *He is a very tall man.*
Repeat: è un uomo molto alto *He is a very tall man.*

English: Woman
Italian: *Donna*

Repeat: *Donna*

Spell: D-o-n-n-a

Use it in a phrase: è una donna intelligente *She is a smart woman*
Repeat: è una donna intelligente *She is a smart woman*

English: Boy/Girl
Italian: *Ragazzo/ragazza*

Repeat: *Ragazzo/ragazza*

Spell: *R-a-g-a-z-z-o/a*

Use it in a phrase: Come si chiama quel ragazzo? *What's that boy's name?*
Repeat: Come si chiama quel ragazzo? *What's that boy's name?*

English: Child
Italian: *bambino/bambina*

Repeat: *bambino/bambina*

Spell: b-a-m-b-i-n-o/a

Use it in a phrase: Ha una bambina di due anni *She has a two year old girl*
Repeat: Ha una bambina di due anni *She has a two year old girl*

English: Father
Italian: *padre*

Repeat: *padre*

Spell: p-a-d-r-e

Use it in a phrase: Mio padre ha quarant'anni *My dad is 40 years old*
Repeat: Mio padre ha quarant'anni *My dad is 40 years old*

English: Mother
Italian: madre

Repeat: *madre*

Spell: m-a-d-r-e

Use it in a phrase: Mia madre si chiama Roberta *My mother's name is Roberta*
Repeat: Mia madre si chiama Roberta *My mother's name is Roberta*

English: Son/Daughter
Italian: figlio/figlia

Repeat: figlio/figlia

Spell: f-i-g-l-i-o/a

Use it in a phrase: Suo figlio non è venuto *His son didn't come*
Repeat: Suo figlio non è venuto *His son didn't come*

English: Brother
Italian: *Fratello*

Repeat: *Fratello*

Spell: f-r-a-t-e-l-l-o

Use it in a phrase: Non ho un fratello *I don't have a brother*
Repeat: Non ho un fratello *I don't have a brother*

English: Sister
Italian: *sorella*

Repeat: *sorella*

Spell: s-o-r-e-l-l-a

Use it in a phrase: Sua sorella è una cantante *His sister is a singer*
Repeat: Sua sorella è una cantante *His sister is a singer*

English: Husband
Italian: *marito*

Repeat: *marito*

Spell: m-a-r-i-t-o

Use it in a phrase: Tuo marito arriva dopo? *Is your husband coming later?*
Repeat: Tuo marito arriva dopo? *Is your husband coming later?*

English: Wife
Italian: *moglie*

Repeat: *moglie*

Spell: m-o-g-l-i-e

Use it in a phrase: Mia moglie è fantastica *My wife is amazing*
Repeat: Mia moglie è fantastica *My wife is amazing*

English: Friend
Italian: *amico/amica*

Repeat: *amico/amica*

Spell: a-m-i-c-o/a

Use it in a phrase: è amico di tua sorella, lo conosci? *He is a friend of your sister, do you know him?*
Repeat: è amico di tua sorella, lo conosci? *He is a friend of your sister, do you know him?*

2.3 Days of the week and time expressions

Making appointments and planning your trip will be much easier if you are aware of how to do it in Italian. The following section of words is going to help you ask what time it is and at what time something will happen, when you are going to meet someone or do a certain activity.

English: Monday
Italian: *lunedì*

Repeat: *lunedì*

Spell: l-u-n-e-d-ì

Use it in a phrase: lunedì vado dal parrucchiere. *Monday I am going to the hairdresser.*
Repeat: lunedì vado dal parrucchiere. *Monday I am going to the hairdresser.*

English: Tuesday
Italian: *Martedì*

Repeat: *Martedì*

Spell: m-a-r-t-e-d-ì

Use it in a phrase: Martedì ci vediamo per un caffè. *Tuesday we are meeting to get a coffee.*
Repeat: Martedì ci vediamo per un caffè. *Tuesday we are meeting to get a coffee.*

English: Wednesday
Italian: *Mercoledì*

Repeat: *Mercoledì*

Spell: m-e-r-c-o-l-e-d-ì

Use it in a phrase: Sei libero mercoledì sera? *Are you free on Wednesday evening?*

Repeat: Sei libero mercoledì sera? *Are you free on Wednesday evening?*

English: Thursday
Italian: *Giovedì*

Repeat: *Giovedì*

Spell: g-i-o-v-e-d-ì

Use it in a phrase: Giovedì è il mio compleanno. *My birthday is on thursday.*
Repeat: Giovedì è il mio compleanno. *My birthday is this thursday.*

English: Friday
Italian: *venerdì*

Repeat: *venerdì*

Spell: v-e-n-e-r-d-ì

Use it in a phrase: andiamo a ballare venerdì? *Let's go clubbing this Friday?*
Repeat: andiamo a ballare venerdì? *Let's go clubbing this Friday?*

English: Saturday
Italian: *Sabato*

Repeat: *Sabato*

Spell: s-a-b-a-t-o

Use it in a phrase: ci siamo conosciuti sabato scorso. *We met last saturday.*
Repeat: ci siamo conosciuti sabato scorso. *We met last saturday.*

English: Sunday
Italian: *domenica*

Repeat: *domenica*

Spell: d-o-m-e-n-i-c-a

Use it in a phrase: Ogni domenica vado alla messa. *Every Sunday I go to the mass.*
Repeat: Ogni domenica vado alla messa. *Every Sunday I go to the mass.*

English: Today
Italian: *Oggi*

Repeat: *Oggi*

Spell: o-g-g-i

Use it in a phrase: Oggi non vado a scuola. *Today I am not going to school*
Repeat: Oggi non vado a scuola. *Today I am not going to school*

English: Tomorrow
Italian: *Domani*

Repeat: *Domani*

Spell: d-o-m-a-n-i

Use it in a phrase: Domani non vengo, ci vediamo la prossima volta. *I am not coming tomorrow, I'll see you next time.*
Repeat: Domani non vengo, ci vediamo la prossima volta. *I am not coming tomorrow, I'll see you next time.*

English: The day after tomorrow
Italian: *Dopodomani*

Repeat: *Dopodomani*

Spell: d-o-p-o-d-o-m-a-n-i

Use it in a phrase: Dopodomani è giovedì. *The day after tomorrow is a thursday.*
Repeat: Dopodomani è giovedì. *The day after tomorrow is a thursday.*

English: Yesterday
Italian: *Ieri*

Repeat: *Ieri*

Spell: i-e-r-i

Use it in a phrase: Ieri ci siamo visti a lavoro. *Yesterday I saw him at work.*
Repeat: Ieri ci siamo visti a lavoro. *Yesterday I saw him at work.*

English: When?
Italian: *Quando?*

Repeat: *Quando?*

Spell: q-u-a-n-d-o?

Use it in a phrase: Quando facciamo colazione? *When are we having breakfast?*
Repeat: Quando facciamo colazione? *When are we having breakfast?*

English: What time is it?
Italian: *Che ore sono?*

Repeat: *Che ore sono?*

Spell: c-h-e o-r-e s-o-n-o?

Use it in a phrase: Sono in ritardo. Che ore sono? *I am late. What time is it?*
Repeat: Sono in ritardo. Che ore sono? *I am late. What time is it?*

English: It's ____ (time)
Italian: *Sono le ____*

Repeat: *Sono le ____*

Spell: s-o-n-o l-e ____

Use it in a phrase: Sono le 09:30, devi andare! *It's 09:30 a.m., you have to go!*
Repeat: Sono le 09:30, devi andare! *It's 09:30 a.m., you have to go!*

English: Now
Italian: *Adesso*

Repeat: *Adesso*

Spell: a-d-e-s-s-o

Use it in a phrase: Adesso siamo amici. *We are friends now.*
Repeat: Adesso siamo amici. *We are friends now.*

English: Soon
Italian: *Presto*

Repeat: *Presto*

Spell: p-r-e-s-t-o

Use it in a phrase: Presto dovrò andare in areoporto. *Soon I'll have to go to the airport.*
Repeat: Presto dovrò andare in areoporto. *Soon I'll have to go to the airport.*

English: After
Italian: *Dopo*

Repeat: *Dopo*

Spell: d-o-p-o

Use it in a phrase: Dopo cena andrò ad una festa. *After dinner I'll go to a party*
Repeat: Dopo cena andrò ad una festa. *After dinner I'll go to a party*

English: Week
Italian: *Settimana*

Repeat: *Settimana*

Spell: s-e-t-t-i-m-a-n-a

Use it in a phrase: La settimana di Natale è la più bella. *The Christmas week is the best one.*
Repeat: La settimana di Natale è la più bella. *The Christmas week is the best one.*

English: Month
Italian: *Mese*

Repeat: *Mese*

Spell: m-e-s-e

Use it in a phrase: A fine mese parto per Milano. *At the end of the month I'll leave for Milan.*
Repeat: A fine mese parto per Milano. *At the end of the month I'll leave for Milan.*

English: Year
Italian: *Anno*

Repeat: *Anno*

Spell: a-n-n-o

Use it in a phrase: L'anno della mia nascita è il 1980. *My birth year is 1980.*
Repeat: L'anno della mia nascita è il 1980. *My birth year is 1980.*

English: Day
Italian: *Giorno*

Repeat: *Giorno*

Spell: g-i-o-r-n-o

Use it in a phrase: Il giorno del mio compleanno voglio divertirmi. *The day of my birthday I want to have fun.*
Repeat: Il giorno del mio compleanno voglio divertirmi. *The day of my birthday I want to have fun.*

English: Hour
Italian: *Ora*

Repeat: *Ora*

Spell: o-r-a

Use it in a phrase: A che ora parte il treno? *At what time does the train leave?*
Repeat: A che ora parte il treno? *At what time does the train leave?*

English: Second
Italian: *Secondo*

Repeat: *Secondo*

Spell: s-e-c-o-n-d-o

Use it in a phrase: è passato un secondo fa. *He passed a second ago.*
Repeat: è passato un secondo fa. *He passed a second ago.*

English: Minute
Italian: *Minuto*

Repeat: *Minuto*

Spell: m-i-n-u-t-e

Use it in a phrase: Arriverà tra qualche minuto. *He will arrive in a few minutes.*
Repeat: Arriverà tra qualche minuto. *He will arrive in a few minutes.*

English: Morning
Italian: *Mattina*

Repeat: *Mattina*

Spell: m-a-t-t-i-n-a

Use it in a phrase: Questa mattina non abbiamo fatto colazione. *This morning we didn't have breakfast.*
Repeat: Questa mattina non abbiamo fatto colazione. *This morning we didn't have breakfast.*

English: Afternoon
Italian: *Pomeriggio*

Repeat: *Pomeriggio*

Spell: p-o-m-e-r-i-g-g-i-o

Use it in a phrase: Ti va di bere un caffè oggi pomeriggio? *Do you feel like getting a coffee together this afternoon?*
Repeat: Ti va di bere un caffè oggi pomeriggio? *Do you feel like getting a coffee together this afternoon?*

English: Evening
Italian: *Sera*

Repeat: *Sera*

Spell: s-e-r-a

Use it in a phrase: Sta sera non sono libero. *I am not free tonight.*
Repeat: Sta sera non sono libero. *I am not free tonight.*

English: Night
Italian: *Notte*
Repeat: *Notte*

Spell: n-o-t-t-e

Use it in a phrase: La scorsa notte non ho dormito. *Last night I didn't sleep*
Repeat: La scorsa notte non ho dormito. *Last night I didn't sleep*

2.4 Months and seasons

Knowing the words for months and seasons will help you plan your visit in Italy, a country in which there's plenty of seasonal events, both natural and man-made, such as markets, festivals and parades. Most of the fruit and vegetables Italy is famous for are also seasonal, so if you are planning to have a foodie excursion, make sure you are going to actually find the product.

English: January
Italian: *Gennaio*
Repeat: *Gennaio*

Spell: g-e-n-n-a-i-o

Use it in a phrase: Gennaio è il primo mese dell'anno. *January is the first month of the year*
Repeat: Gennaio è il primo mese dell'anno. *January is the first month of the year*

English: February
Italian: *Febbraio*
Repeat: *Febbraio*

Spell: f-e-b-b-r-a-i-o

Use it in a phrase: Febbraio è il mese del mio compleanno. *February is the month of my birthday.*
Repeat: Febbraio è il mese del mio compleanno. *February is the month of my birthday.*

English: March
Italian: *Marzo*
Repeat: *Marzo*

Spell: m-a-r-z-o

Use it in a phrase: A marzo inizia la primavera. *Spring begins in march.*

Repeat: A marzo inizia la primavera. *Spring begins in march.*

English: April
Italian: *Aprile*
Repeat: *Aprile*

Spell: a-p-r-i-l-e

Use it in a phrase: La mia laurea è ad aprile. *My graduation is in April.*
Repeat: La mia laurea è ad aprile. *My graduation is in April.*

English: May
Italian: *Maggio*
Repeat: *Maggio*

Spell: m-a-g-g-i-o

Use it in a phrase: A maggio andrò in vacanza. *I will go on holiday in may.*
Repeat: A maggio andrò in vacanza. *I will go on holiday in may.*

English: June
Italian: *Giugno*
Repeat: *Giugno*

Spell: g-i-u-g-n-o

Use it in a phrase: Ci vediamo in giugno! *I will see you in June!*
Repeat: Ci vediamo in giugno! *I will see you in June!*

English: July
Italian: *Luglio*
Repeat: *Luglio*

Spell: l-u-g-l-i-o

Use it in a phrase: Luglio non è il mese più caldo. *July isn't the warmest month.*

Repeat: Luglio non è il mese più caldo. *July isn't the warmest month.*

English: Agust
Italian: *Agosto*
Repeat: *Agosto*

Spell: a-g-o-s-t-o

Use it in a phrase: Ad agosto andiamo al mare. *In August we'll go to the beach.*
Repeat: Ad agosto andiamo al mare. *In August we'll go to the beach.*

English: September
Italian: *Settembre*
Repeat: *Settembre*

Spell: s-e-t-t-e-m-b-r-e

Use it in a phrase: A settembre inizia la scuola. *School starts in september.*
Repeat: A settembre inizia la scuola. *School starts in september.*

English: October
Italian: *Ottobre*
Repeat: *Ottobre*

Spell: o-t-t-o-b-r-e

Use it in a phrase: Ottobre è il mese di halloween. *October is the month of Halloween.*
Repeat: Ottobre è il mese di halloween. *October is the month of Halloween.*

English: November
Italian: *Novembre*
Repeat: *Novembre*

Spell: n-o-v-e-m-b-r-e

Use it in a phrase: A novembre mia madre verrà in visita. *My mom will come to visit in November.*
Repeat: A novembre mia madre verrà in visita. *My mom will come to visit in November.*

English: December
Italian: *Dicembre*
Repeat: *Dicembre*

Spell: d-i-c-e-m-b-r-e

Use it in a phrase: A dicembre andremo a sciare. *We'll go ski in December.*
Repeat: A dicembre andremo a sciare. *We'll go ski in December.*

English: Winter
Italian: *Inverno*
Repeat: *Inverno*

Spell: i-n-v-e-r-n-o

Use it in a phrase: In inverno fa freddo qui. *During winter here it gets really cold.*
Repeat: : In inverno fa freddo qui. *During winter here it gets really cold.*

English: Spring
Italian: *Primavera*
Repeat: *Primavera*

Spell: p-r-i-m-a-v-e-r-a

Use it in a phrase: I fiori e le piante sono bellissimi in primavera. *Flowers and plants are beautiful in spring.*
Repeat: I fiori e le piante sono bellissimi in primavera. *Flowers and plants are beautiful in spring.*

English: Autumn
Italian: *Autunno*
Repeat: *Autunno*

Spell: a-u-t-u-n-n-o

Use it in a phrase: L'autunno è la mia stagione preferita. *Autumn is my favorite season.*
Repeat: L'autunno è la mia stagione preferita. *Autumn is my favorite season.*

English: Summer
Italian: *Estate*
Repeat: *Estate*

Spell: e-s-t-a-t-e

Use it in a phrase: L'estate è molto umida nel mio Paese. *Summer is very humid in my Country.*
Repeat: L'estate è molto umida nel mio Paese. *Summer is very humid in my Country.*

3. Health

There is nothing worse than a medical emergency to ruin your plans and your trip: dealing with doctors, hospitals and health care that you are not familiar with can only make the unpleasant experience of being sick even worse. So, aside planning for our health-care before leaving, what can we do in order to make a potential emergency not as scary and much easier to handle? Learn a few Italian terms related to health and emergencies: enough to allow you to express yourself should something happen during your trip.

Knowing how to communicate a state of discomfort and to ask for a certain medicine, exam or professional will help you in any circumstance of emergency, disease and difficulty.

3.1 Emergencies

English: Hospital
Italian: *Ospedale*
Repeat: *Ospedale*

Spell: o-s-p-e-d-a-l-e

Use it in a phrase: *Mi porti all'ospedale!* Bring me to the hospital!
Repeat: *Mi porti all'ospedale!* Bring me to the hospital!

English: Doctor
Italian: *Dottore*
Repeat: *Dottore*

Spell: d-o-t-t-o-r-e

Use it in a phrase: Dove posso trovare un dottore? *Where can I find a doctor?*
Repeat: Dove posso trovare un dottore? *Where can I find a doctor?*

English: Pharmacy
Italian: *Farmacia*
Repeat: *Farmacia*

Spell: f-a-r-m-a-c-i-a

Use it in a phrase: Ho bisogno di una farmacia. *I need a pharmacy.*
Repeat: Ho bisogno di una farmacia. *I need a pharmacy.*

English: Firefighters
Italian: *Vigili del fuoco*
Repeat: *Vigili del fuoco*

Spell: v-i-g-i-l-i d-e-l f-u-o-c-o

Use it in a phrase: Qualcuno chiami i vigili del fuoco! *Someone call the firefighters!*
Repeat: Qualcuno chiami i vigili del fuoco! *Someone call the firefighters!*

English: Police
Italian: *Polizia*
Repeat: *Polizia*

Spell: p-o-l-i-z-i-a

Use it in a phrase: Dove si trova la centrale di polizia? *Where can I find the police central?*
Repeat: Dove si trova la centrale di polizia? *Where can I find the police central?*

English: Ambulance
Italian: *Ambulanza*
Repeat: *Ambulanza*

Spell: a-m-b-u-l-a-n-z-a

Use it in a phrase: Sta passando un'ambulanza. *An ambulance is passing by.*
Repeat: Sta passando un'ambulanza. *An ambulance is passing by.*

English: Translator
Italian: *Traduttore*
Repeat: *Traduttore*

Spell: t-r-a-d-u-t-t-o-r-e

Use it in a phrase: Sei un traduttore? *Are you a translator?*
Repeat: Sei un traduttore? *Are you a translator?*

English: Embassy
Italian: *Ambasciata*
Repeat: *Ambasciata*

Spell: a-m-b-a-s-c-i-a-t-a

Use it in a phrase: L'ambasciata Americana è lì. *The American embassy is there.*
Repeat: L'ambasciata Americana è lì. *The American embassy is there.*

English: Consulate
Italian: *Consolato*
Repeat: *Consolato*

Spell: c-o-n-s-o-l-a-t-o

Use it in a phrase: Dove si trova il consolato Australiano? *Where is the Australian consulate?*
Repeat: Dove si trova il consolato Australiano? *Where is the Australian consulate?*

English: Taxi
Italian: *Taxi*
Repeat: *Taxi*

Spell: t-a-x-i

Use it in a phrase: Puoi chiamarmi un taxi? *Can you call me a taxi?*
Repeat: Puoi chiamarmi un taxi? *Can you call me a taxi?*

English: Thief
Italian: *Ladro*
Repeat: *Ladro*

Spell: l-a-d-r-o

Use it in a phrase: C'è un ladro sull'autobus! *There's a thief on the bus!*
Repeat: C'è un ladro sull'autobus! *There's a thief on the bus!*

English: Phone
Italian: *Telefono*
Repeat: *Telefono*

Spell: T-e-l-e-f-o-n-o

Use it in a phrase: Puoi prestarmi il tuo telefono? *Can I borrow your phone?*
Repeat: Puoi prestarmi il tuo telefono? *Can I borrow your phone?*

English: Phone
Italian: *Telefono*
Repeat: *Telefono*

Spell: T-e-l-e-f-o-n-o

Use it in a phrase: Puoi prestarmi il tuo telefono? *Can I borrow your phone?*
Repeat: Puoi prestarmi il tuo telefono? *Can I borrow your phone?*

4. Going places

Travelling around Italy will probably mean use some forms of transportation, such as trains, busses, underground, a rented car, or a plane. It will also mean following directions and getting lost once in a while, as well as finding hotels, restaurants, museums and bathrooms. Knowing how to go around in Italy without having to find someone that understands your own language, will save you time and troubles. It might even get you into closer contact with the locals, who will always be very adamant to help and support you however they can. The following word sections will contain all the terms and expressions you may need while travelling across the beautiful regions and cities of the Italian peninsula.

English: Lost
Italian: *Perso*
Repeat: *Perso*

Spell: P-e-r-s-o

Use it in a phrase: Mi sono perso. *I got lost.*
Repeat: Mi sono perso. *I got lost.*

English: Map
Italian: *Mappa*
Repeat: *Mappa*

Spell: M-a-p-p-a

Use it in a phrase: Ha una mappa del luogo? *Do you have a map of the place?*
Repeat: Ha una mappa del luogo? *Do you have a map of the place?*

English: Bathroom
Italian: *Bagno*
Repeat: *Bagno*

Spell: B-a-g-n-o

Use it in a phrase: Posso usare il bagno? *Can I use the bathroom?*
Repeat: Posso usare il bagno? *Can I use the bathroom?*

English: Bank
Italian: *Banca*
Repeat: *Banca*

Spell: B-a-n-c-a

Use it in a phrase: Dov'è la banca più vicina? *Where is the closest bank?*
Repeat: Dov'è la banca più vicina? *Where is the closest bank?*

English: ATM
Italian: *Bancomat*
Repeat: *Bancomat*

Spell: B-a-n-c-o-m-a-t

Use it in a phrase: Devo prelevare soldi al bancomat. *I need to take out cash at the ATM.*
Repeat: Devo prelevare soldi al bancomat. *I need to take out cash at the ATM.*

English: Gas station
Italian: *Benzinaio*
Repeat: *Benzinaio*

Spell: B-e-n-z-i-n-a-i-o

Use it in a phrase: Oggi passiamo dal benzinaio. *Today we are going to the gas station.*
Repeat: Oggi passiamo dal benzinaio. *Today we are going to the gas station.*

English: Supermarket
Italian: *Supermercato*
Repeat: *Supermercato*

Spell: S-u-p-e-r-m-e-r-c-a-t-o

Use it in a phrase: C'è un supermercato da queste parti? *Is there a supermarket around here?*
Repeat: C'è un supermercato da queste parti? *Is there a supermarket around here?*

English: Bus stop
Italian: *Fermata del bus*
Repeat: *Fermata del bus*

Spell: F-e-r-m-a-t-a d-e-l b-u-s

Use it in a phrase: Mi accompagni alla fermata del bus? *Can you bring me to the bus stop?*
Repeat: Mi accompagni alla fermata del bus? *Can you bring me to the bus stop?*

English: Underground station
Italian: *Fermata della metro*
Repeat: *Fermata della metro*

Spell: F-e-r-m-a-t-a d-e-l-l-a m-e-t-r-o

Use it in a phrase: Qual è la fermata della metro più vicina? *Which is the closest underground station?*
Repeat: Qual è la fermata della metro più vicina? *Which is the closest underground station?*

English: Restaurant
Italian: *Ristorante*
Repeat: *Ristorante*

Spell: R-i-s-t-o-r-a-n-t-e

Use it in a phrase: Troviamo un ristorante vicino all'albergo. *Let's find a restaurant close to the hotel.*
Repeat: Troviamo un ristorante vicino all'albergo. *Let's find a restaurant close to the hotel.*

English: Mall
Italian: *Centro commerciale*
Repeat: *Centro commerciale*

Spell: C-e-n-t-r-o c-o-m-m-m-e-r-c-i-a-l-e

Use it in a phrase: Voglio fare shopping. Andiamo al centro commerciale? *I want to shop: let's go to the mall?*
Repeat: Voglio fare shopping. Andiamo al centro commerciale? *I want to shop: let's go to the mall?*

English: Tourist information office
Italian: *Ufficio di informazioni turistico*
Repeat: *Ufficio di informazioni turistico*

Spell: U-f-f-i-c-i-o d-i i-n-f-o-r-m-a-z-i-o-n-i t-u-r-i-s-t-i-c-o.

Use it in a phrase: Possiamo chiedere all'ufficio di informazioni turistico. *We can ask at the touristic information office.*
Repeat: Possiamo chiedere all'ufficio di informazioni turistico. *We can ask at the touristic information office.*

English: Library
Italian: *Biblioteca*
Repeat: *Biblioteca*

Spell: B-i-b-l-i-o-t-e-c-a

Use it in a phrase: Puoi trovare quel libro in biblioteca. *You can find that book in the library.*
Repeat: Puoi trovare quel libro in biblioteca. *You can find that book in the library.*

English: Book shop
Italian: *Libreria*
Repeat: *Libreria*

Spell: L-i-b-r-e-r-i-a

Use it in a phrase: Ho visto una libreria quando siamo passati in macchina. *I saw a book shop when we passed with the car.*
Repeat: Ho visto una libreria quando siamo passati in macchina. *I saw a book shop when we passed with the car.*

English: Gym
Italian: *Palestra*
Repeat: *Palestra*

Spell: P-a-l-e-s-t-r-a

Use it in a phrase: C'è una palestra nell'albergo? *Is there a gym in the hotel?*
Repeat: C'è una palestra nell'albergo? *Is there a gym in the hotel?*

English: Tobacco shop
Italian: *Tabaccaio*
Repeat: *Tabaccaio*

Spell: T-a-b-a-c-c-a-i-o

Use it in a phrase: Hai visto un tabaccaio qui intorno? *Did you see a tobacco place around here?*
Repeat: Hai visto un tabaccaio qui intorno? *Did you see a tobacco place around here?*

English: Veterinarian
Italian: *Veterinario*
Repeat: *Veterinario*

Spell: V-e-t-e-r-i-n-a-r-i-o

Use it in a phrase: Devo portare il mio cane dal veterinario. *I have to bring my dog to the veterinarian office.*
Repeat: Devo portare il mio cane dal veterinario. *I have to bring my dog to the veterinarian office.*

English: Newspaper stand
Italian: *Edicola*
Repeat: *Edicola*

Spell: E-d-i-c-o-l-a

Use it in a phrase: Posso comprare i biglietti all'edicola? *Can I buy the tickets at the newspaper stand?*

Repeat: Posso comprare i biglietti all'edicola? *Can I buy the tickets at the newspaper stand?*

English: Post office
Italian: *Ufficio postale*
Repeat: *Ufficio postale*

Spell: U-f-f-i-c-i-o p-o-s-t-a-l-e

Use it in a phrase: Devo spedire una lettera. Dove si trova l'ufficio postale? *I need to send a letter. Where is the post office?*
Repeat: Devo spedire una lettera. Dove si trova l'ufficio postale? *I need to send a letter. Where is the post office?*

English: Park
Italian: *Parco*
Repeat: *Parco*
Spell: P-a-r-c-o

Use it in a phrase: Andiamo a fare una passeggiata al parco. *Let's go take a walk in the park.*
Repeat: Andiamo a fare una passeggiata al parco. *Let's go take a walk in the park.*

English: Cinema
Italian: *Cinema*
Repeat: *Cinema*
Spell: C-i-n-e-m-a

Use it in a phrase: Andiamo a vedere un film al cinema. *Let's go see a movie at the cinema.*
Repeat: Andiamo a vedere un film al cinema. *Let's go see a movie at the cinema.*

English: Docks
Italian: *Porto*
Repeat: *Porto*
Spell: P-o-r-t-o

Use it in a phrase: Il porto è lontano dall'albergo. *The docks are far from the hotel.*
Repeat: Il porto è lontano dall'albergo. *The docks are far from the hotel.*

English: How do you get to ___?
Italian: *Come si arriva a ___?*
Repeat: *Come si arriva a ___?*
Spell: C-o-m-e s-i a-r-r-i-v-a a ___?

Use it in a phrase: Come si arriva alla stazione? *How do you get to the station?*
Repeat: Come si arriva alla stazione? *How do you get to the station?*

English: Train station
Italian: *Stazione dei treni*
Repeat: *Stazione dei treni*
Spell: S-t-a-z-i-o-n-e d-e-i t-r-e-n-i

Use it in a phrase: Ci vediamo alla stazione dei treni quando arriva. *We'll meet at the train station when he arrives.*
Repeat: Ci vediamo alla stazione dei treni quando arriva. *We'll meet at the train station when he arrives.*

English: Airport
Italian: *Aeroporto*
Repeat: *Aeroporto*
Spell: A-e-r-o-p-o-r-t-o

Use it in a phrase: Partiamo dall'aeroporto della città. *We will leave from the city's airport.*
Repeat: Partiamo dall'aeroporto della città. *We will leave from the city's airport.*

English: Can you recommend a good ___
Italian: Ci può raccomandare un buon ___
Repeat: Ci può raccomandare un buon ___
Spell: C-i p-u-ò r-a-c-c-o-m-a-n-d-a-r-e u-n b-u-o-n ___

Use it in a phrase: Ci può raccomandare un buon ristorante? *Can you recommend us to a good restaurant?*
Repeat: Ci può raccomandare un buon ristorante? *Can you recommend us to a good restaurant?*

English: Bar, cafè
Italian: *bar*
Repeat: *bar*
Spell: b-a-r

Use it in a phrase: Conosci qualche buon bar? *Do you know any good bar?*
Repeat: Conosci qualche buon bar? *Do you know any good bar?*

English: Restaurant
Italian: *Ristorante*
Repeat: *Ristorante*
Spell: R-i-s-t-o-r-a-n-t-e

Use it in a phrase: Abbiamo mangiato al ristorante. *We at the restaurant.*
Repeat: Abbiamo mangiato al ristorante. *We at the restaurant.*

English: Hotel
Italian: *Albergo*
Repeat: *Albergo*
Spell: A-l-b-e-r-g-o

Use it in a phrase: Torniamo in albergo. *Let's go back to the hotel.*
Repeat: Torniamo in albergo. *Let's go back to the hotel.*

English: Touristic attraction
Italian: *Attrazione turistica*
Repeat: *Attrazione turistica*
Spell: A-t-t-r-a-z-i-o-n-e t-u-r-i-s-t-i-c-a

Use it in a phrase: Qual è l'attrazione turistica più lontana? *Which is the furthest touristic attraction?*
Repeat: Qual è l'attrazione turistica più lontana? *Which is the furthest touristic attraction?*

English: Historical site
Italian: *Sito storico*
Repeat: *Sito storico*
Spell: S-i-t-o s-t-o-r-i-c-o

Use it in a phrase: Siamo al sito storico. Vieni? *We are at the historical site. Are you coming?*
Repeat: Siamo al sito storico. Vieni? *We are at the historical site. Are you coming?*

English: Museum
Italian: *Museo*
Repeat: *Museo*
Spell: M-u-s-e-o

Use it in a phrase: Il museo è molto interessante. *The museum is very interesting.*
Repeat: Il museo è molto interessante. *The museum is very interesting.*

5. Accomodation

Whether you are looking for a hotel room, a bed and breakfast or a camping spot, you will need to know the basic terms you'll use to look for the perfect accommodation. The following terms and expressions will help you find and book your room, assist you during your stay and give you all the weapons you may need to complain about anything.

There's a multitude of hotels, b&bs and other solutions for tourists in Italy, as tourism is a big part of the Country's economy. However, if you are planning to travel during hot dates, we recommend you book with plenty of advance, seen as the best deals will quickly disappear and the prices will increase.

5.1 Looking for accommodation

Looking for an accommodation in Italy should be done in advance, especially if you intend on staying in a b&b or a hotel. You might be able to book on the spot at a hostel, but you could also risk not to find a bed. Looking for accommodation can be easily done through plenty of websites, but if you are looking for accommodation only after arriving in Italy, you will need to use these terms.

English: Where can I find ____?
Italian: *Dove posso trovare ____?*
Repeat: *Dove posso trovare ____?*
Spell: D-o-v-e p-o-s-s-o t-r-o-v-a-r-e ____?

Use it in a phrase: Dove posso trovare un museo? *Where can I find a museum?*
Repeat: Dove posso trovare un museo? *Where can I find a museum?*

English: Room for rent
Italian: *Camera in affitto*
Repeat: *Camera in affitto*
Spell: C-a-m-e-r-a i-n a-f-f-i-t-t-o

Use it in a phrase: Avete una camera in affitto? *Do you have a room for rent?*
Repeat: Avete una camera in affitto? *Do you have a room for rent?*

English: Hostel
Italian: *Ostello*
Repeat: *Ostello*
Spell: O-s-t-e-l-l-o

Use it in a phrase: C'è un ostello che mi può raccomandare? *Is there a hostel you can recommend me?*
Repeat: C'è un ostello che mi può raccomandare? *Is there a hostel you can recommend me?*

English: Camping ground
Italian: *Campeggio*
Repeat: *Campeggio*
Spell: C-a-m-p-e-g-g-i-o

Use it in a phrase: Non sono mai stato in campeggio. *I have never been camping.*
Repeat: Non sono mai stato in campeggio. *I have never been camping.*

6. Eating out

Italy is famous for its many delicacies and typical dishes. During your stay in the Country, you will definitely try pizza, pasta, many desserts and other typical products, therefore you need to know how to book a table, order your food, order drinks, pay and complain if you need to. Remember the words section about allergies? Go back to refresh your memories and order what you want to eat without risking your health.

6.1 Ordering food

Depending on the region and city you are visiting, there is going to be a lot of delicious dishes and products to try. Polenta is from Bergamo, wine is great in Veneto, Ascoli is known for Olive all'Ascolana, and in Naples you'll find the best pizza ever. This is why we recommend you ask for the specialties of the restaurant and the typical dish of the city. However, if you find something irresistible on the menu, in the next section you will learn how to order food from a menu. You will also learn how to explain what you don't eat, ask for advices and say that you are allergic to something.

English: Menu
Italian: *Menù*
Repeat: *Menù*
Spell: M-e-n-ù

Use it in a phrase: Mi può portare un menu? *Can you bring me a menu?*
Repeat: Mi può portare un menu? *Can you bring me a menu?*

English: Order
Italian: *Ordinare*
Repeat: *Ordinare*
Spell: O-r-d-i-n-a-r-e

Use it in a phrase: Possiamo ordinare? *Can we order?*
Repeat: Possiamo ordinare? *Can we order?*

English: Specialty
Italian: Specialità
Repeat: Specialità
Spell: S-p-e-c-i-a-l-i-t-à

Use it in a phrase: Qual è la vostra specialità? *Which is your specialty?*
Repeat: Qual è la vostra specialità? *Which is your specialty?*

English: Allergic
Italian: *Allergico*
Repeat: *Allergico*
Spell: A-l-l-e-r-g-i-c-o

Use it in a phrase: Sono allergico al pesce. *I am allergic to fish.*
Repeat: Sono allergico al pesce. *I am allergic to fish.*

English: to eat
Italian: *Mangiare*
Repeat: *Mangiare*
Spell: M-a-n-g-i-a-r-e

Use it in a phrase: Cosa vuoi mangiare? *What do you want to eat?*
Repeat: Cosa vuoi mangiare? *What do you want to eat?*

English: Starters
Italian: *Antipasti*
Repeat: *Antipasti*
Spell: A-n-t-i-p-a-s-t-i

Use it in a phrase: Avete degli antipasti di carne? *Do you serve meat appetizers?*
Repeat: Avete degli antipasti di carne? *Do you serve meat appetizers?*

English: Main dish
Italian: *Portata principale*
Repeat: *Portata principale*
Spell: P-o-r-t-a-t-a P-r-i-n-c-i-p-a-l-e

Use it in a phrase: La portata principale è inclusa? *Is the main dish included?*
Repeat: La portata principale è inclusa? *Is the main dish included?*

English: Desserts
Italian: *Dolci*
Repeat: *Dolci*
Spell: D-o-l-c-i

Use it in a phrase: Quali dolci servite? *Which desserts do you serve?*
Repeat: Quali dolci servite? *Which desserts do you serve?*

English: Salad
Italian: *Insalata*
Repeat: *Insalata*
Spell: I-n-s-a-l-a-t-a

Use it in a phrase: Vorrei un'insalata. *I would like a salad.*
Repeat: Vorrei un'insalata. *I would like a salad.*

English: Soup
Italian: *Zuppa*
Repeat: *Zuppa*
Spell: Z-u-p-p-a

Use it in a phrase: Vorrei una zuppa di verdure. *I would like a vegetable soup.*
Repeat: Vorrei una zuppa di verdure. *I would like a vegetable soup.*

English: Meat
Italian: *Carne*
Repeat: *Carne*
Spell: C-a-r-n-e

Use it in a phrase: Avete carne di agnello? *Do you serve lamb meat?*
Repeat: Avete carne di agnello? *Do you serve lamb meat?*

English: Pork
Italian: *Maiale*
Repeat: *Maiale*
Spell: M-a-i-a-l-e

Use it in a phrase: Non voglio carne di maiale. *I don't want pork meat.*
Repeat: Non voglio carne di maiale. *I don't want pork meat.*

English: Beef
Italian: *Manzo*
Repeat: *Manzo*
Spell: M-a-n-z-o

Use it in a phrase: Solo carne di manzo, grazie. *Only beef, thank you.*
Repeat: Solo carne di manzo, grazie. *Only beef, thank you.*

English: Chicken
Italian: *Pollo*
Repeat: *Pollo*
Spell: P-o-l-l-o

Use it in a phrase: Vorrei del petto di pollo. *I would like some chicken breast.*
Repeat: Vorrei del petto di pollo. *I would like some chicken breast.*

English: Seafood
Italian: *Frutti di mare*
Repeat: *Frutti di mare*
Spell: F-r-u-t-t-i d-i m-a-r-e

Use it in a phrase: Avete i migliori frutti di mare. *You serve the best seafood.*
Repeat: Avete i migliori frutti di mare. *You serve the best seafood.*

English: Fish
Italian: *Pesce*
Repeat: *Pesce*
Spell: P-e-s-c-e

Use it in a phrase: Non abbiamo ancora mangiato pesce. *We still didn't eat fish.*
Repeat: Non abbiamo ancora mangiato pesce. *We still didn't eat fish.*

English: Salt
Italian: *Sale*
Repeat: *Sale*
Spell: S-a-l-e

Use it in a phrase: Manca il sale. *It needs more salt.*
Repeat: Manca il sale. *It needs more salt.*

English: Pepper
Italian: *Pepe*
Repeat: *Pepe*
Spell: p-e-p-e

Use it in a phrase: Posso avere il pepe? *Can I have the pepper?*
Repeat: Posso avere il pepe? *Can I have the pepper?*

English: Bread
Italian: *Pane*
Repeat: *Pane*
Spell: P-a-n-e

Use it in a phrase: Voglio comprare del pane fresco. *I want to buy fresh baked bread.*
Repeat: Voglio comprare del pane fresco. *I want to buy fresh baked bread.*

English: Icecream
Italian: *Gelato*
Repeat: *Gelato*
Spell: G-e-l-a-t-o

Use it in a phrase: Andiamo a prendere un gelato. *Let's go get an icecream.*
Repeat: Andiamo a prendere un gelato. *Let's go get an icecream.*

English: Cake
Italian: *Torta*
Repeat: *Torta*
Spell: T-o-r-t-a

Use it in a phrase: Vorrei una torta al limone. *I would like a lemon cake.*
Repeat: Vorrei una torta al limone. *I would like a lemon cake.*

English: Chocolate
Italian: *Cioccolato*
Repeat: *Cioccolato*
Spell: C-i-o-c-c-o-l-a-t-o

Use it in a phrase: Hai provato la crostata al cioccolato? *Did you try the chocolate pie?*
Repeat: Hai provato la crostata al cioccolato? *Did you try the chocolate pie?*

English: Biscuits
Italian: *Biscotti*
Repeat: *Biscotti*
Spell: B-i-s-c-o-t-t-i

Use it in a phrase: Ci hanno portato caffè e biscotti. *They brought us coffees and biscuits.*
Repeat: Ci hanno portato caffè e biscotti. *They brought us coffees and biscuits.*

English: Enjoy your meal!
Italian: *Buon appetito!*
Repeat: *Buon appetito!*
Spell: B-u-o-n a-p-p-e-t-i-t-o

Use it in a phrase: Mangiamo! Buon appetito! *Let's eat! Enjoy your meal!*
Repeat: Mangiamo! Buon appetito! *Let's eat! Enjoy your meal!*

6.2 Ordering drinks

The most typical Italian drink is wine, particularly famous in certain areas of the country. Wine will usually be served by the glass, half a liter, a liter or a bottle. While in certain parts of Italy drinking tap water is possible, it is recommended to drink bottled water. Coffee is also a very typical beverage in Italy, where it is consumed as an espresso. It is usually consumed multiple times a day and after the meals. Following, you will find the terms and expressions you'll need to order drinks at the restaurant.

English: Sparkling water
Italian: Acqua frizzante
Repeat: Acqua frizzante
Spell: A-c-q-u-a f-r-i-z-z-a-n-t-e

Use it in a phrase: *Ci porta dell'acqua frizzante?. Can you bring us some sparkling water?*
Repeat: *Ci porta dell'acqua frizzante?. Can you bring us some sparkling water?*

English: Still water
Italian: *Acqua naturale*
Repeat: *Acqua naturale*
Spell: A-c-q-u-a n-a-t-u-r-a-l-e

Use it in a phrase: Anzi, acqua naturale, grazie! *Actually, still water please!*
Repeat: Anzi, acqua naturale, grazie! *Actually, still water please!*

English: Beer
Italian: *Birra*
Repeat: *Birra*
Spell: B-i-r-r-a

Use it in a phrase: Vuoi bere una birra? *Do you want to drink a beer?*
Repeat: Vuoi bere una birra? *Do you want to drink a beer?*

English: Bottle
Italian: *Bottiglia*
Repeat: *Bottiglia*
Spell: B-o-t-t-i-g-l-i-a

Use it in a phrase: Scegli la bottiglia che vuoi comprare. *Choose the bottle you want to buy.*
Repeat: Scegli la bottiglia che vuoi comprare. *Choose the bottle you want to buy.*

English: White wine
Italian: *Vino bianco*
Repeat: *Vino bianco*
Spell: V-i-n-o b-i-a-n-c-o

Use it in a phrase: Ci porti un bicchiere di vino bianco. *Bring us a glass of white wine.*
Repeat: Ci porti un bicchiere di vino bianco. *Bring us a glass of white wine.*

English: Red wine
Italian: *Vino rosso*
Repeat: *Vino rosso*
Spell: V-i-n-o r-o-s-s-o

Use it in a phrase: Il vino rosso è migliore! *The red wine is better!*
Repeat: Il vino rosso è migliore! *The red wine is better!*

English: Coffee
Italian: *Caffè*
Repeat: *Caffè*
Spell: C-a-f-f-è

Use it in a phrase: Vorresti un caffè? *Would you like a coffee?*
Repeat: Vorresti un caffè? *Would you like a coffee?*

English: Tea
Italian: *Tè*

Repeat: *Tè*
Spell: T-è

Use it in a phrase: Preferirei un tè grazie! *I would rather have a tea, thank you!*
Repeat: Preferirei un tè grazie! *I would rather have a tea, thank you!*

English: Liqueur
Italian: *Liquore*
Repeat: *Liquore*
Spell: L-i-q-u-o-r-e

Use it in a phrase: Vorrei un liquore dopo pranzo! *I would like some liqueur after lunch!*
Repeat: Vorrei un liquore dopo pranzo! *I would like some liqueur after lunch!*

English: Cocktail
Italian: *Drink*
Repeat: *Drink*
Spell: D-r-i-n-k

Use it in a phrase: Posso avere un drink analcolico? *Can I have an alcohol-free cocktail?*
Repeat: Posso avere un drink analcolico? *Can I have an alcohol-free cocktail?*

English: Juice
Italian: *Succo*
Repeat: *Succo*
Spell: S-u-c-c-o

Use it in a phrase: Vuoi un succo all'arancia o alla pera? *Would you like an orange juice or a pear juice?*
Repeat: Vuoi un succo all'arancia o alla pera? *Would you like an orange juice or a pear juice?*

English: Smoothie
Italian: *Frullato*

Repeat: *Frullato*
Spell: F-r-u-l-l-a-t-o

Use it in a phrase: Abbiamo preso un frullato alla fregola. *We took a strawberry smoothie.*
Repeat: Abbiamo preso un frullato alla fregola. *We took a strawberry smoothie.*

English: Hot chocolate
Italian: *Cioccolata calda*
Repeat: *Cioccolata calda*
Spell: C-i-o-c-c-o-l-a-t-a c-a-l-d-a

Use it in a phrase: Prendi una cioccolata calda, è deliziosa! *Have a hot chocolate, it is delicious!*
Repeat: Prendi una cioccolata calda, è deliziosa! *Have a hot chocolate, it is delicious!*

English: Camomile tea
Italian: *Camomilla*
Repeat: *Camomilla*
Spell: C-a-m-o-m-i-l-l-a

Use it in a phrase: Posso avere una camomilla? Ho mal di pancia. *Can I have a chamomile tea? I have a stomachache.*
Repeat: Posso avere una camomilla? Ho mal di pancia. *Can I have a chamomile tea? I have a stomachache.*

English: Herbal tea
Italian: *Tisana*
Repeat: *Tisana*
Spell: T-i-s-a-n-a

Use it in a phrase: Hai preso una tisana calda? *Did you have a warm herbal tea?*
Repeat: Hai preso una tisana calda? *Did you have a warm herbal tea?*

Conclusions

Is it difficult to learn Italian?

Italian, when compared with other languages, is considered one of the easiest to learn, but like any new skill, Italian may seem difficult at first.

The Italian language is a Romance language and belongs to the same family as Spanish, French, Catalan and Portuguese. Languages belonging to the Romance family have similarities in sounds, structure and vocabulary. Italian remains the Romance language closest to Latin, the language of ancient Rome. Thanks to the Latin roots, and being a Romance language, if you know another language of the same family or Latin, learning Italian becomes a much faster and easier process due to the fact that many words and grammatical structures are similar . Those interested in subjects such as music or cooking may already have knowledge of many basic Italian words. Italian became formalized as a language at the beginning of the 14th century and part of the credit goes to the famous Italian poet Dante Alighieri who, through his works, has combined his Tuscan dialect with the southern languages of Sicily and other regions. Subsequently, the Tuscan dialect became the common language with which Italians could understand and converse throughout the peninsula.

The difficulties of the Italian language

Some languages are intrinsically difficult to learn, but Italian has the advantage that it reads as it is written being a phonetic language. But there are some important things to note because Italian grammar can be complex for some foreign students. Compared to the English language there are many more articles, there are seven verbal forms, many tenses, conjugations, and a huge amount of irregular verbs that require effort to be memorized. There are plurals that do not follow the rules such as: Arm (masculine), which becomes arms (feminine); egg (masculine), whose plural is feminine. In addition, there are nouns that maintain the same form both in the singular and in the plural, such as those ending in consonant, or with the accent on the last vowel, and abbreviations. Other rules seem to have no apparent logic because certain things are said in a certain way (idiomatic expressions) and their meaning must be learned. However, all this does not hinder the learning of Italian. But learning a second language also depends on the level of knowledge of the grammar and structure of the first language. This has a direct effect on the way in which the second language is absorbed, therefore much of the learning of Italian as a second language has to do with knowledge of the grammar and structure of your mother tongue. So, the better your knowledge of the mother tongue, the better you learn Italian.

Understanding and knowing "the parts of the speech" helps a lot.

Reading and listening is based on the knowledge of words. Students who want to understand what they read or what they listen to must know a vast vocabulary not only in Italian but also in their mother tongue. For example, a student is unable to read simple sentences or short paragraphs in Italian if he does not know the meaning or function of the words he is reading in his native language. Therefore, knowing the meaning of vocabulary is essential for learning the language at a basic and medium level.

To teach vocabulary, many teachers use the communicative method that emphasizes vocabulary and sentences without giving too much importance to grammar. The communicative method is, in fact, one of the best for learning to speak a foreign language, it is a fluent teaching system designed with the specific objective of making people speak, without emphasis on grammar. But the ability of grammatical analysis, knowing the parts of the learning speech, is very useful not only for understanding listening and reading, but also for writing.

The parts of the speech are those that express the meaning of the sentences and are fundamental in the teaching and learning of all languages at medium and advanced levels. In Italian, the parts of speech are divided into nine parts of which five are called variables, in that they have a flexion: noun, adjective, article, pronoun, and verb; four invariables: adverb, preposition, conjunction and interjection. Learning them improves through reading and writing, listening and speaking.

The issues with pronunciation

As a general rule of pronunciation (there are exceptions), in Italian the emphasis is on the penultimate syllable of the word. If the emphases must be placed at the end of the word, an accent is placed on the last vowel, for example: città, caffè, università, perchè, ect. Many students have a problem pronouncing double consonants; when a consonant is double the intonation of the word must be different from when it appears by itself: a double consonant means that the previous vowel must be longer, with more bending over it. Two common words that South Americans don't pronounce well are spaghetti and ricotta. Furthermore, many students have difficulties with the pronunciation of "t" and "r" and with the sound of "gli", which does not exist in English (the closest sound is in "million"). Other difficulties are noted with the consonant "c" because it is pronounced hard, like the English "k" (as in kart), before o, u, but before e and i is pronounced like the English "ch". The consonant "g" also acts similarly.

You will need time and patience to learn, but nothing is impossible if you apply yourself.

www.ingramcontent.com/pod-product-compliance
Lightning Source LLC
Chambersburg PA
CBHW030916080526
44589CB00010B/334